My Snail

My Snail

by Herbert H. Wong
and Matthew F. Vessel

Illustrated by
Jean Day Zallinger

Addison-Wesley

Science Series for the Young

Level A:
My Ladybug
My Goldfish
Our Tree
Our Terrariums

Level AA:
My Plant
My Snail
Our Caterpillars
Our Earthworms

Level B:
Pond Life: Watching Animals Find Food
Animal Habitats: Where Can Red-Winged Blackbirds Live?
Plant Communities: Where Can Cattails Grow?
Pond Life: Watching Animals Grow Up

An Addisonian Press Book

Addison-Wesley Publishing Company, Inc.
Reading, Massachusetts 01867
Printed in the United States of America

WZ/WZ 9/76 08762

Library of Congress Cataloging in Publication Data

Wong, Herbert H
My snail.

"An Addisonian Press book."
SUMMARY: A simple description of the characteristics of both land and water snails.
1. Snails—Juvenile literature. [1. Snails]
I. Vessel, Matthew F., joint author. II. Zallinger, Jean Day. III. Title.
QL430.4.W66 593'.3 75-29368
ISBN 0-201-08762-6

SCIENCE SERIES FOR THE YOUNG

Look at this thing!
What is it?
It is a snail. Is it dead?

It looks dead.
It does not move.
Where is its head?

Maybe the head is in the shell.
The snail may not be dead.
Maybe it only plays dead.
How can we tell?

Snails like leaves.
We can put it on some leaves.
Will it move?
Will it come out of its shell?
We will go away.
It may come out then.

How did the snail get here?
Look! Here is a snail trail!
It is white and shiny.
Maybe it tells where the snail comes and goes.

The shiny trail goes up. Then down.
Now it goes out.
Down it goes.
Down, down, down. Way down.
Where does it go then?
We will go out and see.

Here is the shiny trail.
The trail comes all the way down.
It is pretty dark and damp here.

Look at all the leaves.
And all the funny holes in the leaves!
Hey, here is a big snail.
Did it make the holes in the leaves?
Look! The trail goes by the holes.

What did you two find?
Snails? Snails are fun to find.
We will look for snails, too.
Here is one under the leaves.
And there is one on the damp leaves.

Look how all the snails make sticky trails.
The snail moves here and there.
It is dark here. Can the snail see where it goes?
The snail has four feelers on its head.
The two big feelers move up and down.
They move this way and that way.
What do the big feelers do? And the little feelers?

So a snail can "smell" with its little feelers!
But, do snails hear?
I see no ears.
Can they hear with no ears?

We can tap and see.
Tap! Tap! Tap!
The snail stops. Does it hear?
But there are no ears.
Tap! Tap! Tap!
The feelers go into its head.
Hey! A snail does feel the taps.

Here is a funny snail down here in the dark.
It has feelers and a big foot.
It is yellow.
And it feels sticky, too.
Where is its shell?
It is a slug. A slug has no shell.
A slug is not like a snail.

Here is something new by this snail.
It looks like eggs.
Snail eggs!

Feel my snail. Pet it.
It feels damp. It feels sticky, too.
Hey, the feelers go in fast!
The foot goes into the shell, too.
Now we cannot see the snail at all.

The snail cannot be dead.
But all we can see is the shell.
The shell is like a snail house.
This snail is like the snail at home.
Go get that snail. We want to see it.

You see, our snail is not dead.
It eats the leaves.
Hey, look at its foot.
The foot moves in a funny way.

We must tell Mike.
Mike's home is out of the city.
But Mike's Dad comes into the city.
Maybe Mike can find a snail, too.
And we can have a snail race!
Mike's snail and our city snail.
That will be fun!

Here comes Mike's Dad.
With a box! A box!
It must be Mike's snail.
I want to see what it looks like.

Hey, Mike's snail is in water!
What a surprise!
It must be a water snail.
And our snails are land snails.
Land snails cannot race water snails.
No snail race now!

What do we do with Mike's snail?
Mike says to put it in a water habitat.
A water habitat?
Yes, he must want the snail in water.
He put leaves in here, too.

The water snail has a foot.
And feelers? I see two, not four like our land snails.
Its shell is not like the shell of our snails.
I do not see snail trails.
So does it make trails?
Yes, this water snail moves like our land snails.
But we cannot see the trails in the water.

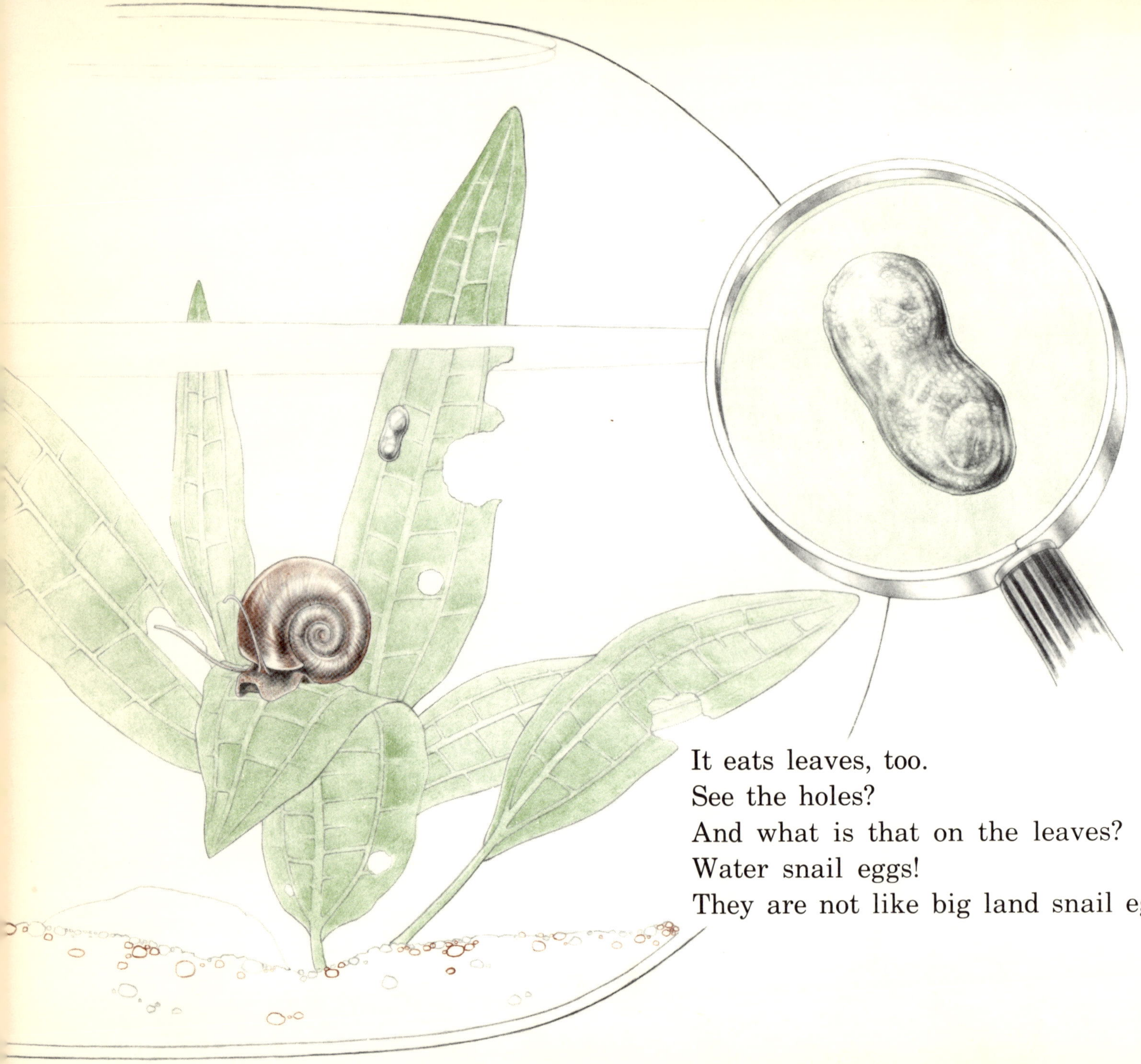

It eats leaves, too.
See the holes?
And what is that on the leaves?
Water snail eggs!
They are not like big land snail eggs.

Mike must see one of our snails.
We will get one to him!
Mike's Dad can take it.
What a surprise! It will please Mike.
We will put some of our leaves in, too.
Mike can put the land snail in a land habitat.

Mike will not have a snail race.
Land snails cannot race water snails.
But Mike will have fun with our snail.
He will find the shiny snail trail.
And a big shell.
And not two feelers, but four.

Land snails are like water snails in some ways.
All snails have a head, a foot, and feelers.
Land snails and water snails have shells, too.
But land snails must have a land habitat.
And water snails must have a water habitat.

About the Authors

Herbert H. Wong is well known as an author of science books for children and teachers, as a science education, environmental studies, and jazz education consultant, and as an educator. He is the Principal of the University of California Laboratory School, Washington Elementary, in Berkeley, California. Dr. Wong is active in many environmental education and science curriculum development projects and pilot programs. He holds a degree in Zoology and also Ed.D. from the University of California.

Matthew F. Vessel, Associate Dean of the School of Science of San Jose State University, is a biologist, an author, editor, and consultant in science and education. He is a Fellow of the American Association for the Advancement of Science. An active member of many other professional science and education societies, Dr. Vessel attended St. Cloud State University and the University of Minnesota. He holds the Ph.D. from Cornell University.

About the Artist

Jean Day Zallinger is a sensitive artist with many children's books to her credit. She formerly used her talents to illustrate two other books for Addison-Wesley, *The Mayfly* by Ross E. Hutchins, and *Fishes That Hide* by Alan Mark Fletcher. Again, in *My Snail*, she has added beauty and fascination with her delightful drawings. Mrs. Zallinger, a mother of three, is a graduate of Yale's School of Fine Arts.